LUTHER
FROM INNER CITY

BY BRUMSIC BRANDON, JR.

PAUL S. ERIKSSON, INC.
New York

Paul S. Eriksson, Inc., 119 West 57th Street, N.Y., N.Y. 10019. Published simultaneously in the Dominion of Canada by Fitzhenry & Whiteside, Ltd., Don Mills, Ontario. Library of Congress Catalog Card Number: 74-93235. SBN 8397-5650-X. Design by Brumsic Brandon, Jr. Manufactured in the United States of America

First Printing

TO
RITA,
LINDA,
BRUMSIC III,
BARBARA,
MOM
AND
POP

PROTEST
MEETING
EVERY MONDAY
MARTIN LUTHER KING
MEMORIAL CENTER

-AND HE STARTED NON-VIOLENT DEMONSTRATIONS!
THAT'S RIGHT, PEE WEE, MARTIN LUTHER KING WAS A GREAT MAN - THAT'S WHY I WAS NAMED AFTER HIM!
BUT YOU'RE TOO YOUNG TO - HOW DO YOU KNOW ABOUT NON-VIOLENT DEMONSTRATIONS?
MY MAMA TOLD ME! SHE OUGHTA KNOW - SHE GOT BEAT UP IN ONE!
©1969
BRANDON JR

THERE ARE THREE BROKEN WINDOWS IN OUR APARTMENT!
THERE'S A BIG HOLE IN THE BATHROOM CEILING!
THERE'S A CRACK IN THE WALL IN THE KITCHEN!
©1969 BRANDON JR
I WONDER IF THAT'S THE OPEN HOUSING I HEAR SO MUCH ABOUT!

GREAT GOOGLY WOOGLY! WHAT HAPPENED, HARDCORE?
EVERYTIME MY MAMA HEARS ME TALKING LIKE THE BIG GUYS ON THE CORNER - - -
- - - SHE SLAPS ME RIGHT IN THE MOUTH!
IS THAT WHAT LIVING HAND TO MOUTH MEANS, LUTHER?

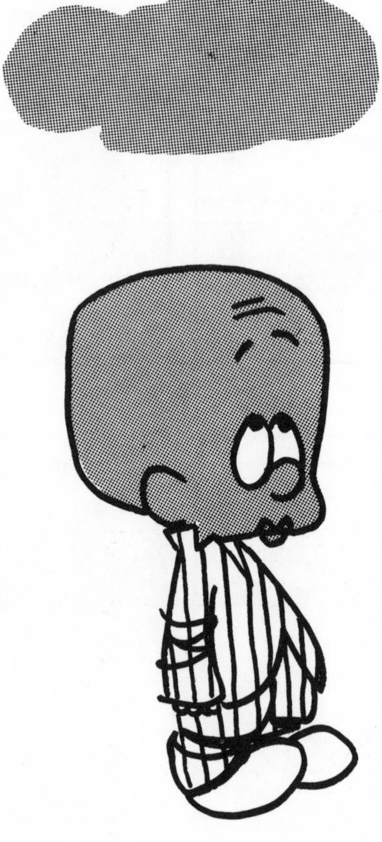

OH OH, IT'S STARTING TO RAIN, PEE WEE!
WHY DOES IT RAIN, LUTHER?
IT RAINS TO MAKE THINGS GROW - LIKE BUSHES AND TREES AND GRASS!
WHY DOES IT RAIN HERE? - EVERYTHING'S SIDEWALK!
©1969

MIRROR, MIRROR ON THE WALL...

WHERE WERE YOU YESTERDAY, OREO?
I HAD TO STAY INSIDE BECAUSE I FELL DOWN AND HURT MY KNEE!
WHICH ONE ?
I CAN'T TELL ANYMORE...
MY MOTHER PUT A FLESH COLORED BAND-AID ON IT!
©1969
BRANDON JR

GRRRRR

MAN, I'M HUNGRY! I HOPE WE DON'T HAVE LEFTOVERS TODAY!
WHAT ARE LEFTOVERS, LUTHER?
FOOD THAT WAS LEFT OVER FROM ANOTHER MEAL!
OH!
PEE WEE, COME ON UP HERE AND EAT YOUR DINNER, BOY!
YES MAMA!
WHAT DO YOU CALL LEFT OVER LEFTOVERS, LUTHER?
©1969
BRANDON JR

MERCY! WHAT HAPPENED TO YOU?
I GOT INTO A FIGHT DOWN THE STREET!
THAT'S AWFUL! NOW YOUR FOLKS WILL MOVE AWAY FROM THIS NEIGHBORHOOD!
WHO BEAT YOU UP ?
MY SISTER !
©1969
BRANDON-JR

LET'S GO TO YOUR HOUSE AND LOOK AT THOSE OLD MOVIE MAGAZINES!
I KNEW IT - I KNEW IT!
WHAT?
I KNEW WHEN PEOPLE LIKE HARDCORE MOVED INTO THIS NEIGHBORHOOD THINGS WOULD START GOING DOWNHILL!
JUST LOOK AT THAT!
©1969 BRANDON JR

CAN YOU TELL ME ABOUT THE HAWKS AND THE DOVES, LUTHER?
WELL, THE DOVES JUST WANT THE WAR TO **END**-
-BUT THE HAWKS WANT TO **WIN** THE WAR!
SO THE HAWKS MUST NOT BE FIGHTING THE WAR ON POVERTY!
©1969 BRANDON JR

URBAN
ENEWAL
PROJECT

IT MAKES ME SAD TO SEE THEM TEAR DOWN THE BUILDING WHERE I WAS BORN!
I'D LIKE TO SEE THAT HAPPEN TO THE PLACE WHERE I WAS BORN!
WHERE WERE YOU BORN, HARDCORE?
—IN A POLICE CAR?!
©1969 B BRANDON JR

WERE YOU REALLY BORN IN A POLICE CAR, HARDCORE?
YEP, THAT'S WHY COPS DON'T LIKE ME, OREO!
THAT'S SILLY, POLICEMEN ARE OUR FRIENDS IN BLUE!
OH YEAH?
AFTER THE COP HELD ME UP LIKE THIS AND WHACKED ME ON MY BACK—
©1969 B. BRANDON JR
MY MOTHER ACCUSED HIM OF POLICE BRUTALITY!

IF YOU WANNA PLAY COPS AND ROBBERS WITH US, YOU GOTTA BE THE COP, PEE WEE!
OK
STOP THAT DANCING, BOY!
WHAT'S ON YOUR MIND?! MY NAME IS MARY FRANCIS AND I'M A GIRL!
HARDCORE TOLD ME COPS CALL EVERYBODY "BOY"!
©1969 BRANDON JR

HI LILY! DO YOU WANT TO JUMP ROPE WITH ME?
NO, OREO...
MY MOTHER TOLD ME NOT TO PLAY WITH YOU!
BUT WHY? WHAT HAPPENED? WHAT'S WRONG?
WHAT DID I DO?
NOTHING, MOM THINKS I'M COMING DOWN WITH A BAD COLD!
©1969 BRANDON JR

WHAT A DISGUSTING ANIMAL!
THIS IS OUR CAT! HER NAME IS "PROUD"!
HOW DO YOU KNOW ITS A "HER"!
GEE, I HOPE SO..
MY UNCLE SAID WE DON'T NEED ANYMORE TOMS AROUND HERE!
©1969
BRANDON JR

WHAT'S THE MATTER, PEE WEE?
I'M SUPPOSED TO GET A NEW SUIT!
SO WHY ARE YOU CRYING?
MY BROTHER DIDN'T FINISH OUTGROWING IT YET!
©1962 B. BRANDON JR

HA HA HA
HA HA HA HA HA HA
HA HA HA HA HA HA
HA HA
HA HA
HA
HA
ARE YOU STILL LAUGHING AT THE JOKE HARDCORE TOLD THIS MORNING?
HA HA
YES!
IT WAS CUTE, BUT EVERYBODY ELSE STOPPED LAUGHING A LONG TIME AGO!
©1969 BRANDON JR
I GUESS BLONDES REALLY DO HAVE MORE FUN THAN ANYBODY!
HA HA HA HA HA HA HA HA HA HA

WHAT CAN WE PLAY, OREO?
I CAN'T LILY, I HAVE TO GO HOME!
WANT TO PLAY, PEE WEE?
NOT NOW, I HAVE TO EAT!
PAPER DOLLS?! I CUT THEM OUT A LONG TIME AGO!
JUST WHAT I THOUGHT.. BLONDES DON'T HAVE ANYMORE FUN THAN ANYBODY ELSE!
©1969 B. BRANDON JR

WHY AREN'T YOU PLAYING WITH THE REST OF THE KIDS TODAY, LUTHER?
I AM!
WE'RE PLAYING HOUSE!
WELL WHY ARE YOU HERE AND THE OTHER KIDS ARE WAY DOWN AT THE OTHER END OF THE BLOCK?
I'M THE LANDLORD!
©1969 BRANDON JR

WHAT'S SO FUNNY, YOUNG FELLOW?
HA HA HA HA HA
PEE WEE, HERE, WANTS TO BE PRESIDENT OF THE UNITED STATES!
YOU SHOULDN'T LAUGH, IN THIS COUNTRY EVERY CITIZEN HAS A CHANCE---NO MATTER WHAT HIS RACE, CREED OR COLOR!
BUT LOOK AT HIM, MISTER, HE'S NOT 35 YEARS OLD!
HA HA HA HA!
©1969
6/3
BRANDON JR

DID YOU SEE ALL THOSE PEOPLE WHO CAME TO SEE PEE WEE TODAY?
THEY MUST BE SPENDING THE NIGHT. I DIDN'T SEE THEM LEAVE!
THOSE KIDS SURE LOOK A LOT LIKE PEE WEE!
WELL, HARD CORE-
..THEY MUST BE CLOSE RELATIVES!
TOO CLOSE!

PEE WEE
FOR
PRESIDENT

WHEN I BECOME THE PRESIDENT THINGS ARE GOING TO BE A WHOLE LOT BETTER...
PEOPLE ALL OVER THIS COUNTRY WILL LOVE ME!
I'LL MAKE JUST ONE CAMPAIGN PROMISE... AND I'LL KEEP IT!
ONE MAN, ONE BED!
©1969 . 6/5
BRANDON JR

YESTERDAY THE SNOW WAS WHITE..
..TODAY IT'S BLACK! WHAT HAPPENED TO IT, LUTHER?
©1969 BRANDON JR
I DON'T KNOW IF IT WAS AIR POLLUTION OR BLACK POWER, PEEWEE!

MAN, IT WAS COLD LAST NIGHT!
OUR PLACE WAS SO COLD, I COULDN'T GET TO SLEEP!
I'M STILL COLD! HOW DID YOU MAKE OUT, PEE WEE?
OK
FIVE IN ONE BED HAS ADVANTAGES AT THIS TIME OF YEAR!
©1969
BRANDON JR.

Z

THEN THE GOOD COWBOY, ALL DRESSED IN WHITE, BEAT UP THE BAD MAN, DRESSED IN BLACK—
Z
PEE WEE!
I'VE TOLD YOU BEFORE, YOU CANNOT SLEEP IN THIS CLASSROOM!
I COULD IF SHE'D QUIT YELLING AT ME!
©1969
BRANDON JR

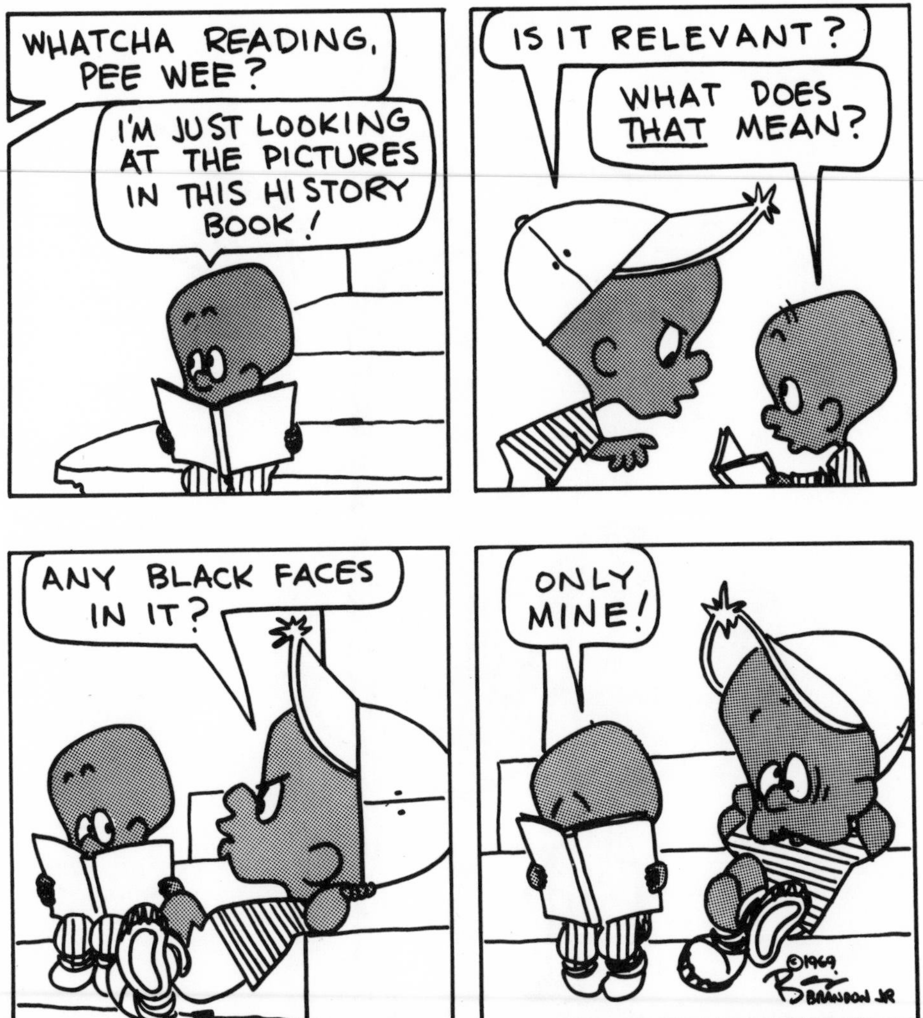
WHATCHA READING, PEE WEE?
I'M JUST LOOKING AT THE PICTURES IN THIS HISTORY BOOK!
IS IT RELEVANT?
WHAT DOES THAT MEAN?
ANY BLACK FACES IN IT?
ONLY MINE!
©1969
B BRANDON JR

SO YOUR CLASS IS GOING TO THE PARK TODAY, PEE WEE?
YES!
HOW FAR IS IT?
OH, ABOUT THREE BLOCKS!
IS THERE A MAILBOX NEAR THE PARK?
I THINK SO, WHY?
I'VE NEVER BEEN SO FAR FROM HOME SO I'D LIKE TO SEND MY MAMA A CARD!

WILL I GET A NEW TEACHER NEXT YEAR, LUTHER?
SURE!
-TEACHERS DON'T STAY AT OUR SCHOOL VERY LONG!
GOOD! I DON'T LIKE MISS BACKLASH—SHE ALWAYS CALLS ME STUPID---
BUT I HEARD NICE TEACHERS SAY CULTURALLY DEPRIVED!
BRANDON JR

MAN, I'M GLAD VACATION TIME IS HERE! WHAT'S BUGGING YOU, LUTHER?
SCHOOL!
WE DON'T GO BACK TO SCHOOL TILL SEPTEMBER! WHY WORRY NOW?
'CAUSE NEXT SEPTEMBER WHEN THE TEACHER SAYS WRITE A STORY ABOUT MY VACATION---
I'LL HAVE TO TURN IN A BLANK PIECE OF PAPER AGAIN!
©1969 BRANDON JR

MY MAMA'S BROTHER DOESN'T WANT ME TO CALL HIM "UNCLE" ANYMORE!
THAT'S A GAS, MAN! THAT MEANS HE KNOWS YOU'RE GROWING UP!
IT MUST MAKE HIM FEEL PRETTY OLD TO HAVE A BIG GUY LIKE YOU CALL HIM UNCLE!
I DON'T THINK THATS IT, HARDCORE— HIS NAME IS TOM!
©1969

HOW COULD YOU BE SO MAD ON SUCH A BEAUTIFUL SUN SHINY DAY, MARY FRANCIS?
THAT STUPID OREO! I OUGHTA GO UPSIDE HER BIG HEAD!
BUT WHY?
WE WERE PLAYING DEMONSTRATION.. BUT LOOK AT HER!
BLACK IS BEAUTIFUL
©1969 B. BRANDON JR